REAL MEALS on 18 WHEELS:

A GUIDE FOR HEALTHY LIVING ON THE HIGHWAY

By

Kathryn Clements, RD
Harriet Hodgson, BS, MA

www.realmealson18wheels.com

REAL MEALS ON 18 WHEELS:
A GUIDE FOR HEALTHY LIVING ON THE HIGHWAY

Copyright 2011 © Kathryn Clements, RD
and Harriet Hodgson, BS, MA
All rights reserved.

ISBN: 1469903881
ISBN-13: 9781469903880

Cover design by Jay Highum, Rochester, Minnesota, USA

Front and back cover photos courtesy of Navistar, Inc.

This book is not intended to serve as a replacement for professional medical care or advice. The information in the guide is based on the Dietary Guidelines for Healthy Americans, and established Standards of Care of the American Dietetic Association, American Heart Association, American Diabetes Association, and American Cancer Society. The authors and publisher specifically disclaim any and all liability arising directly or indirectly from the use or application of any information contained in this book. A health care professional should be consulted regarding a specific situation.

TABLE OF CONTENTS

PREFACE

The poor health of truck drivers is a secret many know and few are willing to talk about. Maybe you're in on the secret. You have no time for physical activity because your schedule is packed. When you're hungry you eat quickly and don't pay attention to the food choices you make. Stress keeps you awake at night and sleepy during the day. You're overweight, have a history of high blood pressure and have been told you are pre-diabetic.

All of these are bad enough, but you also worry about losing your job if you don't pass your next physical.

What can you do? You can read *Real Meals on 18 Wheels* by Kathryn Clements, a registered dietitian, and Harriet Hodgson, a health writer. This guide contains factual information to help you make informed health choices. Despite a copyright date of 2011, the book actually began in the summer of 2005, when the president of a transportation company invited Kathryn to interact with truckers at Driver Appreciation Week activities.

Drivers completed a survey, joined a walking program using pedometers, and read information about meal planning. During the event, Kathryn met personally with drivers and helped them create individual eating plans. Conversations focused on sleeping, physical activity, and lifestyle changes truckers could make to improve their health and live beyond the 60-year life expectancy.

If she was going to work with the trucking industry to promote healthy eating, Kathryn needed to understand what trucking was all about. So she climbed into the cab of a truck, traveled with a commercial driver from Minnesota to North Carolina, and back. You could say her trip was a reality check. Though it wasn't what you go through each day, it helped her understand truckers and the challenges they face.

A year later, Kathryn was invited to share healthy eating information with truckers during New Driver

Orientation. The conversations revealed the personal habits of truckers who have driven millions of accident-free miles and Kathryn learned from their comments.

"I don't want recipes," you're probably muttering, "and I don't want a diet book either." Well, you can relax. *Real Meals on 18 Wheels* isn't a cookbook or a diet book; it's a healthy eating guide. The information in it has survived the tests of time and science. Most of this information comes from your parents and grandparents, people who ate three meals a day, vegetables, fruits, meat, potatoes, and drank milk to satisfy the body's needs.

You have a busy life, so we've made the guide as brief as possible and features include:

- basic nutrition information
- fundamentals of meal planning
- a conversational style.
- truck drivers' real-life experiences
- strategies for lasting change
- Smart Steps you may take.

An audio book will be available soon and we hope you'll listen to it again and again.

Though *Real Meals on 18 Wheels* is geared for truckers, you don't have to be a trucker to benefit from it. The guide will help you if you travel regularly for your job, have an RV, are a week-end tourist, or enjoy day trips. Keep it in the door pocket and refer to it when you stop for food. Share the guide with other drivers, relatives and friends.

We thank all the drivers who shared their experiences with us. We also thank Thomas J. Slavin, Global Safety and Health Director of Navistar, Inc., for providing the front and back cover photos and seed money to launch this project. Tom gave us a helping hand just when we needed it.

We thank Samuel Anderson, President and CEO of Bay and Bay Transportation, for his encouragement and describing our efforts as a "march toward bringing information to help our important, yet unsung, heroes of the highway." Thanks to Gerald Krueger, PhD, CPE, for his help with the sleep chapter. Finally, we thank C. John Hodgson, MD, MPH for reviewing the manuscript.

A healthier life sounds like an impossible goal, but it isn't. If you keep your eyes on the goal, work towards it slowly and steadily, you will reach it. Not only will you feel better, look better, and drive better, you will prolong your life. There is no better day than today – now – this moment – to improve your health. Release the brake and get going!

1
GETTING WHAT YOU WANT AND NEED

Richard wanted to drive a truck for another four years before retiring to his Wisconsin cabin. He had diabetes, high blood pressure, and weighed more than 400 pounds. As you might expect, Richard was angry and resentful about his out-of-control weight, diabetes, and high blood pressure. His doctor had already delivered the death certificate; it just hadn't been recorded at the court house.

Richard was desperate and wanted to live.

A Cherokee Indian, Richard said he wasn't a religious man, but believed everyone had a purpose for living. Since he wasn't ready to die, he began exercising and eating healthier foods. He planned meals and bought food to prepare in his truck while on the road.

Though this required extra effort, Richard was willing to put forth this effort. Day by day, as he ate to satisfy hunger, his confidence grew.

Richard enjoyed the smells and tastes of the meals he cooked. Sometimes he met his need for social contact by sharing the food he cooked on a grill next to his truck. He met his need for physical activity by walking every day. As the months passed and the seasons changed, he gradually increased his walking distance to two miles a day.

Richard literally walked his way to better health.

Three changes – walking, normal eating, enough sleep – made him feel better physically and emotionally. He wasn't as crabby or short-tempered as he used to be and started to enjoy life again. His blood pressure improved, his blood sugar stabilized, his constipation, headaches, and acid reflux lessened. Some medications were reduced and others were discontinued.

A year later, Richard was almost unrecognizable, for he had lost 100 pounds. Thanks to commitment, perseverance, and determination, he was well on his way to fulfilling his wants and needs. Richard is now living his dream, and you can too.

Commercial drivers like you have the ability to meet their wants and needs. It's similar to what you do when a load is dispatched. Mindful of your purpose, you deliver cargo on time, to a specific place, on a specific day. This skill may be applied to daily life.

Think about your wants and needs and list them on paper. Rank them in order of importance. Which one is at the top of your list? Discovering what you want and need is a work in progress. You will start to see things more clearly, feel more in control, and get more joy from life.

SMART STEPS

- ✓ Write your top health goal on a piece of paper and put it where you can see it.
- ✓ Envision how your life would be different if your needs were met.

DEFLATING STRESS

As a licensed commercial driver, you have a long "to do" list that never gets done. You can't seem to let go of the stress and, even worse, you know it. Stress comes with a high price tag, something you also know, and it's the risk of premature death. What you want and need is a reprieve from stress.

Stress can take over your thinking and your life. When you feel stressed or threatened, your brain responds by releasing adrenaline and noradrenalin. Did you know your mind can also counteract stress with a relaxation response? Just as your heart begins to beat rapidly when you're frightened, your mind can consciously slow your heart rate.

Breathing nourishes your body with oxygen, which is transferred from the lungs to the blood-stream and every cell of your body. Oxygen is used to produce energy. Carbon dioxide, the waste product, is carried back to the lungs and exhaled. When you relax, you physically release muscles from habitual, unconscious tension.

Relaxing takes practice and the more you practice it, the easier it becomes. Knowing how to relax will reduce your stress significantly. But learning to create inner quiet is a new experience for many. If you're going to enjoy a healthy balance in your life, this is exactly what you must do. You may wish to explore meditation, mindfulness, repetitive exercise, repetitive prayer, progressive muscle relaxation, yoga stretching, or guided imagery.

Diaphragm breathing also helps you to relax, as these comparisons show. Stress increases your body's metabolism; relaxation decreases it. Stress increases your heart rate; relaxation decreases it. Stress raises your blood pressure; relaxation decreases it. Stress increases your breathing rate; relaxation decreases it. Finally, stress increases your muscle tension; relaxation decreases it.

You may practice diaphragm breathing while sitting, standing, or lying down. Place your hands on your diaphragm, just above your belly button. Slowly take a deep breath, pulling in your diaphragm muscles as you do so, and release it slowly. Your hands will move out as you inhale and move in as you exhale.

Continue your diaphragm breathing and focus your attention on the movement of your hands.

Though random thoughts may distract you and cause shallow breathing, this isn't the time to give up. Return your thoughts to the sound of your breathing and the movement of your hands. As you exhale, imagine the tension draining out of your body from head to toe. Continue this exercise for three or more breaths.

Regular diaphragm breathing can lower your blood pressure 10-15 points. The best thing about diaphragm breathing is that you can do it anywhere. Once you've mastered the technique you can incor-porate it in daily activities. Try taking three or more diaphragm breaths:

- before turning on the engine
- when you stop for a rest break
- when you can't sleep
- when you talk to your dispatcher
- if you're stuck in slow-moving traffic
- while refueling your truck

- when you feel things are getting out of control
- before eating.

Diaphragm breathing can help you control anxiety and tension. This simple stress management tool is as close as your own breath. Use it!

SMART STEPS

✓ Practice diaphragm breathing now and incorporate it into your daily routine.
✓ Practice saying "no" to the things that don't support your wants and needs.

Resource

The Wellness Book: The Comprehensive Guide to Maintaining Health and Treating Stress-Related Illness by Herbert Benson, MD and Eileen M. Stuart, RN.

3
POWER-UP
WITH SLEEP

Humans spend one third of their lives sleeping. But truckers who have tight schedules may become so focused on deadlines they can't sleep, don't get enough sleep, or cut back on sleep. All of these are harmful to health. Adults need seven to nine hours of sleep a night. What does sleep do for you?

Doctors and scientists know a lot about sleep, yet in many ways it is a medical mystery. They do know, however, that sleep helps repair muscles, aids memory, releases hormones that regulate your appetite and growth, and more. A shortage of sleep makes it harder for you to concentrate, gather facts, make decisions, and interact with others.

Most important, lack of sleep impairs driving.

As the National Sleep Foundation explains, our bodies and brains go through distinct sleep stages. During stage one sleep, you're transitioning between being awake and falling asleep. During stage two sleep, your breathing and heart rate are regular and your body temperature drops. Stages three and four sleep are restful and best for your body, lowering blood pressure, relaxing muscles, repairing and growing tissues, and restoring energy.

About 90 minutes after falling asleep your body goes into the REM (random eye movement) dreaming sleep mode. Sleep experts consider this the most restoring period of sleep. Your brain is active, you dream, your eyes shift back and forth, but your body is completely relaxed. Regular sleep helps your immune system and your appetite. Surprisingly, the lack of sleep can make you feel hungry, lead to eating more, and ultimately weight gain.

Diabetes is also affected by a lack of sleep. Sleep experts think regular sleep has a positive effect on glucose control. The less sleep you get, the more apt you are to gain weight. Extra pounds increase the body's resistance to insulin.

Keep in mind that your body has two "lull periods" each day, one usually in mid-afternoon from 1–4 p.m., for about 25 minutes, and again, if you happen to be working or driving in the wee hours of the morning, from 1-4 a.m. During these lull periods you feel drowsy, are less attentive, and would probably like to take a nap and not drive.

Your body physiology may be slightly different than another person's. Some people see themselves as "larks" because they wake up early, perform pretty well during the day, and go to sleep early at night. Other people see themselves as "owls" because they like to wake up later in the morning, work longer days, and go to sleep late. So an "owl's" body rhythms may be about two hours later than a "lark's" rhythms.

The moral of this sleep story: Learn your body's patterns and take extra caution during your lull periods. Working at night when you must, and trying to adjust your sleep pattern to an irregular schedule can lead to alertness problems. A night driving schedule can deprive you of necessary sleep, result in drowsiness, thinking problems, and slower reaction time.

What are the warning signs of sleepiness? Yawning is an obvious sign. Frequent blinking is also a sign and you may close your eyes for a second or two. Keeping your eyes focused becomes difficult. Scariest of all, you may not remember the last few miles of driving.

Sleep specialists have many tips for getting the sleep you need. One tip, not having television in the bedroom, may not get your approval. Watching television while you're in bed doesn't help you get a good night's sleep. In fact, you may program your mind with random ideas, images, and worries. Each day, you can follow these tips from Dr. Gerald Krueger, a noted DOT trucking industry lecturer on commercial driver sleep, alertness and fatigue.

- Try to get seven-to-eight hours of sleep in every 24-hour day.
- Remember, longer sleep sessions restore the brain more than short ones.
- Get at least one continuous four-hour sleep session, preferably at night.
- Augment your sleep periods with naps until you reach seven to eight hours per 24-hour day.
- Take a mid-afternoon nap to help maintain alertness.
- Be mindful of your body's circadian rhythms and take extra caution during the two lull periods each day.

Other health experts think eating a light meal, avoiding spicy foods, caffeine, and nicotine helps to promote sleep.

Sleep apnea, a temporary cessation of breathing, is a concern for many truckers. This medical condition affects their safety and the safety of other drivers. According to recent research, 28–42 percent of all over the road drivers in the US have obstructive sleep apnea. Obstructive sleep apnea happens when the throat muscles relax. Central sleep apnea happens when the brain doesn't send the right signals to the muscles that control breathing. Sleep apnea is diagnosed in a sleep laboratory, under the supervision of a physician. Truckers who use a CPAP (Continuous Positive Airway Pressure) machine report a better night's sleep and improvements in their daily lives.

Regular sleep is one of the best (and free) medicines for commercial drivers. Think about the changes you could make to improve sleep. Just a few changes can give you energy and enthusiasm for the coming day.

SMART STEPS

- ✓ Consider how your life may change if you had more sleep.
- ✓ Add sleep to your trip plan.

Resources

Krueger, Gerald, PhD, CPE

Mayo Clinic website, "Delayed Sleep Phase"

Mayo Clinic website, "10 tips for Better Sleep"

Mayo Clinic website, "Sleep and Diabetes"

National Sleep Foundation website, "What Happens When You Sleep?"

Xerox, "Waking a Sleeping Giant: Obstructive Sleep Apnea and Trucking"

4

GET MOVING, KEEP MOVING

During 2006 Driver Appreciation Activities at a trucking company in Rosemount, Minnesota, drivers and office employees were invited to join in an eight-week walking program using pedometers. The program was based on three key points.

- Help drivers and employees to become more physically active.
- Increase truckers' awareness and responsibility for their health.
- Create a health-friendly workplace.

To encourage 30 minutes of physical activity most days of the week, 500 steps were added to the previous week's walking average. As fall slipped into the chilly days of early winter, the company president monitored the impact of the walking program on employees. Drivers and workers continued to walk regularly and make lifestyle changes.

On the road, concern about your own wellbeing, your loved ones' wellbeing, tight schedules, congested traffic, inclement weather, financial worries, poor eating and sleep habits may rob you of energy. The last thing you want to think about is regular physical activity, yet intellectually, and at some other level, you want more endurance, better balance, flexibility, and strength. You also know daily physical activity would make you feel better.

An important first step to becoming more physically active is to consider how you may benefit from it, tomorrow, next week, next month, and next year. Knowing why it is important is like starting your truck engine. Until you turn the key, nothing is likely to change, and you use the same old excuses – too tired, too busy, too preoccupied – to excuse the lack of physical activity.

Think of the health benefits you would receive if you were more physically active. Do you remember Richard? He wanted to live long enough to retire to his cabin. Every day, he pictured himself sitting comfortably in a boat on a quiet lake and fishing. He pictured himself walking to and from the boat with little or no effort, and climbing into it with relative ease. Richard's desire to change was stronger than his desire to stay the same.

To kick-start your dreams of increasing physical activity, remember some of the activities you enjoyed in the past. Did you dance, bowl, run, swim, hunt, farm, garden, play baseball, basketball, or softball? Did you run and play outside for hours without stopping? How did you feel when you did these things?

Felix had been inactive for years. When he decided to become physically active again, he began with dancing. He turned on the radio and danced beside his truck, positioning his arms as if he was holding the woman of his dreams in his arms. People would smile and wave at him and, though he smiled and waved back, he kept dancing.

You don't have to dance like Felix to be physically active and can do something as simple as walking around your truck. One time around is about 200 feet. You may walk while your truck is being loaded and unloaded. Some drivers walk around roadside stops, city parks and trails. If you're going to be physically active on a regular basis, you need to find something you enjoy.

Jeff, a cross-country runner in high school, added a two-mile run to his daily schedule. Marcus put a bike rack on the back of his truck, and rode it to unwind, stay in shape, and enjoy nature. Larry did calisthenics beside his truck. Archie was preparing to run a marathon in a few months. Arlene used stretchy exercise bands and weights in the safety of her cab.

Commercial driving requires you to sit for hours. Before you begin a regular physical activity program, you need to check your health. Do you have a heart condition? Have you ever felt pain in your chest during physical activity? Do your feet ache? How is your balance? Are any joints bothering you? How long has it been since you were physically active? See your doctor before resuming physical activities if you have any of these health problems.

Regular physical activity helps to keep your muscles strong and your bones aligned. Physical activity can also lift your spirits. There will always be barriers that get in the way of your dreams, but you can achieve them with persistence, planning, and regular physical activity. So get up, get moving, and keep at it!

SMART STEPS

✓ Treat physical activity like an appointment and put it on your schedule.

✓ Be physically active every day for at least 30 minutes.

5
HARNESSING CHANGE

When Kathryn meets with commercial drivers at New Driver Orientation sessions, one of the first questions she asks is, "What do you need from this new work relationship that was missing before?" In a few minutes, Kathryn and the drivers are discussing the choices that affect life in positive and negative ways.

For example, you may feel hungry, but continue driving. Though you monitor the fuel gauge to make sure you have enough fuel, you may ignore the hunger gauge within you, the gauge that tells you your body is running low on fuel. Just as you plan stops to refuel your truck, planning what to eat, when to eat, and how much fuel to consume keeps your body running. You have the power to ignore the old excuses for poor eating, including few choices, high cost, and no time.

Food is your body's fuel. Under normal conditions your fuel supply lasts four-to-six hours, except when you're sleeping. When you ignore your body's hunger message, you're ignoring the fuel gauge wired into your DNA. Wanting to eat when you're hungry answers your body's call for fuel.

Fatigue, frustration, irritability and concentration problems are also symptoms of hunger. Safety and shelter often trump eating in your race to keep the wheels rolling and deliver loads on time. Like safety, eating is essential to your survival. You want to change, but lack of knowledge, lack of motivation, and other barriers keep you stuck in place.

You don't have to be stuck. Behavioral scientists, Drs. James O. Prochaska and Carlo DiClemente, created a wheel of change to demonstrate fluctuating motivation. Prochaska and DiClemente view motivation as an internal state influenced by external factors. Change is a process and it's normal for someone to go around the wheel several times before reaching stable change.

Relapse is part of the wheel and shouldn't be confused with becoming discouraged, demoralized, or bogged down. Keep in mind that different stages of change require different strategies. The circle image may help you move from one stage to another with confidence. As you move through the stages, don't forget to bring your sense of humor with you. It offers shelter when life gets too serious or too critical.

If you have taken the steps cited in previous chapters, you are already starting to harness change. You have started a journey to a healthier, longer life. Understanding the readiness to change will help you on your journey. Which of the following sentences best describes your readiness to change?

- I never considered change.
- I need more information and want to change.
- I need help with motivation.
- I'm working on health changes, but need skills, structure, and support.
- I've made changes and need reinforcement.
- I've made health changes that have lasted for months without major setbacks.

Notes in a diary, numbers on a scale, and results of medical tests may be used to gauge your progress. But lasting change is personal and affects your sense of wellbeing and happiness. Harnessing change is a precious gift you give yourself. Or as one trucker commented, "It's up to me!"

The process of harnessing change isn't as hard as you may think. Each time you pick up a load you know where're you're headed. You navigate your way along highways, through towns and cities, around traffic jams, withstand storms and glaring sun, and other barriers. Reaching your destination hinges upon understanding the changes you need to make to reach your goals.

SMART STEPS

- ✓ Identify your top health goal.
- ✓ Consider what you can do today to reach it.

Resource

The Wellness Book: The Comprehensive Guide to Maintaining Health and Treating Stress-Related Illness by Herbert Benson, MD and Eileen M. Stuart, RN.

6

MASTERING YOUR
MOTIVATION

To live until you're 90, you must make deliberate and purposeful decisions. These decisions are for today, tomorrow, and the future. Though you know this, you may not face health issues and put off decisions. Have you thought about your health wants and needs? Truckers need to be strong and able to move about. You need stamina and resilience as well.

Some commercial drivers want these things without an action plan to achieve them. No doubt you have considered a health plan, retirement plan, or business plan. You have the necessary licenses and permits. What about your life? Have you made a life plan?

Life is like driving a truck and the road ahead leads to your destination. While you're driving, you focus on the road and traffic flow. You look in the rear view mirror to check approaching traffic. Mentally shift gears and think about how you plan to reach your life destination.

According to health experts, 70 percent of the factors and costs that impact health are preventable. Your livelihood as a CLD driver depends on the quality of your life, your mental abilities, physical strength, and more. One change can have a huge impact on your health.

Bobby had yearly physical exam. A smoker for 30 years, he had dull, yellowish skin, a smoker's cough, stained teeth, stained fingers, and unpleasant breath. Climbing in and out of his truck was an effort and walking a flight of stairs to the Safety Director's office was something he avoided. Every year, regular as clockwork, Bobby's doctor advised him to stop smoking.

"I know I should stop," Bobby explained, "but I just can't get motivated."

His doctor gave him a card with the names and contact numbers of smoking cessation clinics. "Stick this in your wallet," he said. "Use it when you're ready."

Staying motivated can be a challenge. Becoming aware of your thoughts, needs and intentions can go a long way in mastering motivation. Intellectually, maintaining motivation means taking responsibility for your choices. Emotionally, mastering motivation hinges on powerful goals – your goals. But motivation can fizzle as you race through life, confront road blocks, and fail to handle stress.

Life is a journey. Motivation is all about making choices that give your life purpose and support this purpose. Looking at yourself honestly, gathering information, developing skills, and revising plans will help you get past barriers and, at the same time, meet your personal needs.

Think of motivation as art and you're the artist. You make choices every day, hour by hour, and minute by minute. These choices help you create a painting of your life. More important, they help you reach your goals, develop self-confidence, and steadiness. These tips will help you harness the motivation inside you.

- Take some responsibility for your health.
- Connect with your feelings.
- Be honest with yourself; no detours, no excuses.
- Confront the barriers in your way.

- Think of ways to improve your health.
- Ask for help if you think you need it.
- Credit yourself for the courage to change.

SMART STEPS

✓ Try some of the tips listed above.
✓ Ask people to stop nagging you because nagging doesn't work.

MOVING BEYOND
BARRIERS

Four real-life stories show how it is possible to move beyond barriers. After 26 years as a computer programming supervisor, Gene walked away from a six-figure salary and generous compensation package to start a new career as an over the road driver. He applied his supervising skills to his new job. Every day, for example, he checked his route and created a plan. He understood the importance of self-care, including nutrition, adequate sleep, and physical activity – things that affected his job.

Because Gene planned for barriers, he was able to avoid or lessen them.

Diabetes was Lorenzo's barrier. He knew he needed to change his eating habits to avoid dips in his blood sugar that zapped his mental alertness, energy, and a feeling that he could eat everything in sight. Lorenzo began to plan menus and purchase food to eat in his truck every four-to-six hours. Between meals, when he felt different inside, he ate a 200-calorie snack to keep his blood sugar stable. These small changes helped him feel better and more in control of his life.

His physician asked Lorenzo to reduce his caffeine intake and he did. This health change had big benefits and, in just a few weeks, his nervousness had almost disappeared. But the big pay-off to all these changes came during his next medical checkup, when his physician told him his A1c had improved from 8.4 mg/dl to 7.0. As Lorenzo continued to make health changes, he noticed his shirts were easier to button and his belt had moved in a couple of notches.

Financial worries were Ben's barrier and he felt he was drowning in them. Each month, he spent hundreds of dollars eating in truck stops, fast food restaurants, and coffee shops. Though he paid five and ten dollars twice a day for snacks, his disappearing money was a mystery. How do you start to move beyond barriers? You start with what you have and Ben had a close friend named Adam. One day, he heard Adam tell another driver that he spent only $150 a month on food to carry in his truck.

This conversation got Ben thinking and he prepared food at home and froze individual servings to take with him. This small step saved Ben hundreds of dollars and he used the money to pay bills. Ben was so encouraged he decided to confront his $7,000-a-year tobacco habit and contacted a quit plan coach. Much to his surprise, he found out that quitting smoking would improve his breathing in a matter of months.

Isolation was Sidney's barrier. Trucking can be a lonely business and to cope with loneliness Sidney stayed in touch with elementary students at a rural Minnesota school. He had been their Trucking Buddy for years and contacted the kids at least once a week via computer. He challenged the kids to learn about the places he had been and the places he was going. The kids' replies made Sidney smile and helped him combat the loneliness and isolation of his job.

What are some other common barriers? Social pressure is one of them. When you go to a safety meeting or Driver Appreciation Week activity you feel like you have to fill your plate out of habit. Grocery shopping is another barrier and you may be an impulse buyer. To control impulse buying, make a grocery list, stick to it, and pay cash for your purchases.

Storing and cooking food can be a daily barrier for commercial drivers. Planning your meals, shopping during your down time, and stopping every few days to restock will help you get past this barrier. Watching for economically priced fruits and vegetables and keeping snacks on hand also helps.

Emotions may be one of the biggest barriers you face. You may eat because you're angry, lonely, tired, or bored. When you find yourself eating, ask yourself if you are really hungry and explore your feelings: anger, loneliness, fatigue, boredom or thirst.

Think about your health barriers. In order to move beyond them, you must be able to name them. Time is a barrier for many truckers. Money is a barrier as well. Lack of knowledge is a third. After you've identified your barriers, take steps to stack the odds in your favor. Start by ignoring slick radio and television ads and getting reliable information from your physician, a registered dietitian, or health coach.

Moving beyond barriers sounds scary and you may wonder if you're up to the challenge. But as you take control of your life again, you'll be able to get past these barriers and continue on your way to a healthier life.

SMART STEPS

- ✓ Make decisions that support your dreams.
- ✓ Give yourself credit for each small success.

EATING TO LIVE

Some drivers live to eat and others eat to live. Which are you? Sensible eating can prolong your life and help you savor the flavors and textures of food. You plan your trip, so you may as well plan the food you eat. The US Government Dietary Guidelines can help you with this planning.

Just as there are often several ways to reach a destination, there are several ways to reach your health goals. But you need patience and the right tools to get there.

First, you need to know about the essential nutrients your body needs for growth, repair, and proper function. Second, you need to know how much energy (calories) your body needs to maintain a healthy weight. Third, you need to recognize hunger, eat until are satisfied, and decide when to stop eating.

What essential nutrients do you need? The US Government set Recommended Daily Allowances (RDAs) for calories and nine essential nutrients: protein, iron, calcium, vitamins A and D, thiamin, riboflavin, niacin and ascorbic acid (vitamin C). If you remember eating meat and potatoes and your mother telling you to "eat your carrots," you may have been on the receiving end of the information in the "Basic Four" food groups. Updated guidelines ask consumers to reduce their consumption of extra calories, fat, cholesterol, and sugar.

Like many truckers, you may rely on a map and compass to reach your destination. A nutrition guide may also help you make eating decisions on the road. You'd be happy if the symptoms of gout, constipation, acid reflux, irritability and that logy feeling went away. Long instructions are a turn-off, but you're interested in a short food plan. Start planning now by reviewing the five food groups and including foods from each one in your plan.

Hold up your hand. Your thumb represents the bread, cereal, rice, grain, and pasta group. Your pointer finger represents the vegetable group. Your middle finger represents the fruit group. Your ring finger represents the milk, yogurt and cheese group. Your pinky finger represents meat, poultry, fish, dried beans, eggs and nuts. Now close your hand around fats, oils, sweets and other foods you want to eat in limited amounts.

To stay healthy, you need to refuel your body with nutrient-rich foods every four-to-six hours. This may sound impossible, but it is possible. To make it happen, you need to plan nutritious meals and snacks for those times when the dinner lights are turned off or the timing is wrong. How much should you eat? To answer this question, use your hand again.

Make a fist. Your closed fist may serve as a guide to check portion sizes. Include food from every group in most of your meals. If you're eating two or more closed fistfuls from one food group, chances are you're eating too much. The trade-off of eating one food and missing others is that you may be eating calorie-dense foods – foods that may not supply your body with the nutrients it needs. As you drive the highways, remember to monitor your hunger. Eat a wide variety of foods until you feel satisfied and stop eating even if you haven't cleaned your plate.

Think about your eating habits and how they compare with your health needs. Don't beat yourself up if your habits need improving. Becoming aware of your food choices is what's important. This awareness brings you closer to your goals and dreams. So when your day or trip ends, give yourself an "atta boy' or "atta girl" for the things you did well. Tomorrow is another day.

SMART STEPS

✓ Be aware of what you eat and drink each day.
✓ Use the worksheet in Appendix A to sharpen your awareness.

9

FOOD IS FUEL

Long before you climb into the cab, you know how far your truck will go on a tank of fuel. Knowing how much fuel (calories) your body needs is just as important. Estimating your daily calorie intake is as easy as reading road signs. Just take your current weight and add a zero to it. This estimate is the number of calories your body needs to maintain your **current** body weight.

To determine how many calories you need to reach or **maintain** a healthy weight, add a zero to what you want your healthy weight to be. Use this number as an estimate to plan meals, menu choices, and snacks.

Do you remember a childhood time when you ate meals every four-to-six hours? You came to the table hungry, ate until you were satisfied, and left the table. Four-to-six hours later you were expected to show up for the next meal. Someone else was probably responsible for fixing these meals, but you are now that someone.

You are responsible for planning what, when and how much you eat.

The food you eat is changed into glucose (blood sugar). This fuel is stored for approximately four-to-six hours in your liver, muscles, and blood. When you over-eat, excess glucose is stored in your body's blood and fat cells. When you were a child, chances are you ate a variety of foods that provided energy from protein, carbohydrates and fats. To keep a healthy weight, there are times when knowing the number of calories in food works in your favor. Calories may also help you plan meals.

How do you plan? Imagine the face of a round clock. Draw an imaginary line between the 12 and the six. At nine, write the word *carbohydrate*. This half of the clock face represents about 50 percent, or the 45–65 percent of carbohydrates recommended by the National Academy of Science Institute of Medicine.

Now draw an imaginary line from the two to the center of the clock, as if you were drawing one of its hands. By the one on your imaginary clock, mentally write the word *protein*, followed by *20 percent*. This represents the Institute of Medicine's recommended protein range of 10–35 percent for daily protein.

Move on to the two and six on the clock. Mentally write the word *fat*, followed by the words less than *30 percent*. According to nutrition experts, meals that have less than 30 percent fat are healthy for you. In fact, your meals should be 40-65 percent carbohydrate and 10-35 percent protein, and less than 30 percent fat. Apply this information to a 2,000 daily calorie intake and the breakdown is:

- 50 percent from carbohydrates, or 1,000 calories
- 20 percent from protein, or 400 calories
- 30 percent or less from fat, or 600 calories.

To figure out how to meet your nutrition needs every four-to-six hours, divide by three. This is the same information used in diabetic meal plans and heart-healthy meal plans.

Aside from water, protein is the most abundant material in your body. It is found in all of your cells and the hemoglobin that carries oxygen in the blood.

Protein provides the code to replicate cells, build muscle and body tissue, and is an important part of insulin, which regulates blood sugar.

Let's take a closer look at protein, carbohydrate and fat, starting with protein. Your body needs a limited amount of protein. Protein contributes four calories per gram. With the exception of a few fruits and vegetables, which are sources of carbohydrates, some protein is provided in most foods. Understanding your protein needs may help you determine which foods to eat to satisfy hunger and meet nutrient needs. The following table shows protein recommendations at various energy (calorie) levels. This information may be useful if you want to know how your food choices compare with needs. See the worksheet in Appendix A for more information.

National Academy of Science Institute of Medicine Dietary Protein Recommendations Based on a 10-35% range of total calories				
If your daily calorie needs are:	1500	2000	2500	3000
Then your protein needs in calories are:	150–525	200–700	250–875	300–1050
Protein in grams are:	38–131	50–175	63–219	75–263

Carbohydrate – a combination of hydrogen, oxygen, and carbon atoms – is the body's primary source of energy, as well as an important source of vitamins, minerals, fiber and antioxidants. These atoms combine to make single sugars, double sugars, starches and fibers. Single sugars, found in fruit, enter your body's energy supply more quickly than double sugars or starches. Over-processed carbohydrates are poor sources of nutrients and these foods are said to have "empty calories." A step in the right direction is to walk past the sugar-laden snack food or beverage display that is calling "buy me, buy me" and choose a healthier snack or drink.

You may be one of the many drivers with diabetes that avoids fruit. To benefit from the abundance of vitamins, minerals, and immunity-fighting properties naturally packed into fruit, include fruit in your daily eating plan. Carbohydrates contribute four per calories per gram. Fruits and vegetables are as essential to healthy eating as putting the key in your truck ignition.

According to the National Academy of Science Institute of Medicine, an acceptable range for carbohydrates is 45–65 percent of your calorie needs. To maintain energy balance, choose fiber-rich foods such as whole grains, vegetables, fruits, cooked dry beans and peas as well as dairy products. The National Academy of Science Institute of Health recommends the following intakes of carbohydrates at various calorie levels.

National Academy of Science Institute of Medicine Dietary Carbohydrate Recommendations Based on a 45–65 % range of total calories				
If your daily calorie needs are:	1500	2000	2500	3000
Then your carbohydrate needs in calories are:	675–975	900–1300	1125–1625	1350–1950
Carbohydrate needs in grams are:	168–244	225–325	281–406	337–487

Fat in the right amount helps your body run smoothly and makes food taste good. In your body, fat helps to build cell walls and membranes, protects your vital organs, and prevents excessive heat loss. But too much of the wrong fats may contribute to health problems, including high blood pressure, heart disease, diabetes, some forms of cancer, and excess body weight. Fat calories add up fast, since they contribute nine calories for every gram of fat you eat.

Your typical fat intake should be less than 30 percent of your diet. Some fats are better choices than others. Saturated fats such as butter, cream, bacon fat, sausage, and fat in beef, chicken, pork and turkey, do the most damage to your body. These fats are called saturated fats and are solid at room temperature. Saturated fat is a villain in the cholesterol battle. Limiting saturated fat, and increasing your intake of fruits and vegetables, will help you keep cholesterol in check.

Unsaturated fats – called monounsaturated and polyunsaturated – are considered safer fats to eat. However, they need to be eaten sparingly. The best sources of monounsaturated fats are plant oils (olive and nut-based), nuts, olives, avocados, seeds, and peanut butter. There is a lot of buzz around omega 3 fatty acids. Provided in polyunsaturated fats, they are believed to have health-promoting properties. Polyunsaturated fats, considered as good sources of omega 3 fatty acids, are liquid or soft at room temperature. They are found in salmon, tuna, herring and mackerel, nuts, almonds, peanuts, walnuts, sesame oil, liquid or soft margarine, and mayonnaise.

The US Government has regulated trans fats out of the American diet. So it's smart to invest your time and energy in improving other areas of health. The following is the National Academy of Science Institute of Medicine recommendation for dietary fat intake. This information completes the trio of where calories are provided in your diet.

National Academy of Science Institute of Medicine Dietary Fat Recommendations Based on less than 30% of total calories				
If your daily calorie needs are:	1500	2000	2500	3000
Then your fat needs in calories are:	500	600	750	900
Fat in grams are:	56	67	83	100

Before you eat, think of the clock image you drew in your mind, and use it to make food choices. Make the best choices for you. In the future, when you climb into the cab, you will feel better about yourself and your choices. Like the right truck fuel, savvy food choices keep your body running well.

SMART STEPS

✓ Calculate your calorie, protein, carbohydrate, and fat needs.

✓ Read product labels and use this information to make healthy choices.

10
ESSENTIAL
NUTRIENTS

Over the years, you have driven millions of accident-free miles, many of them logged in the same truck. You listen constantly for sounds that may indicate an engine malfunction. You top off the gas tank and check the oil regularly. Your truck needs a steady, consistent fuel supply, and so does your body.

Diesel fuel releases potential energy in the form of carbon and hydrogen. In your body, carbohydrates, proteins and lipids (fats) are the fuel sources of potential energy. Carbon, hydrogen, nitrogen, oxygen, phosphorous, and sulfur transform and release energy from food. You may think this is too much information, but understanding amino acids is similar to understanding the hitch on the back of your cab. The trailer can't be connected without a hitch. In your body, amino acids help to connect or release potential energy and they need vitamins to complete the hook-up.

Vitamins take on two forms, water-soluble and fat-soluble. Water-soluble vitamin C and B complex, go about their work freely, moving in and out of your cells. When your body gets more water-soluble vitamins than it needs, excess vitamins are filtered through the kidneys and expelled. Fruits, vegetables and whole grain are sources of vitamins C and B complex. With the exception of avocados, they are fat-free, full of water, and low in calories.

Fat-soluble vitamins A, D, E and K are found in food fats and oils. Because they don't dissolve in water, they need bile for absorption to move through the lymphatic system, where they enter your blood. The blood disperses these vitamins to the liver and fatty tissue and they are stored until needed. Since your body stores these vitamins, you may eat less on some days without ill effects.

Taking vitamin supplements may be your nutrition solution. But there are things to consider, and one is cost. Your body needs more than 27 nutrients and eating balanced meals is the best way to meet this need, not spending hundreds of dollars on vitamins. Then, too, the claims on vitamin bottles may not be true. The supplement industry is big business, and your best interests aren't always on manufacturers' minds.

The best route to follow is your ancestors' habit of eating fruits, vegetables and grains in moderate amounts. Foods in these groups are rich in water-soluble C, B and complex B vitamins. You may consume foods rich in vitamin C, the one that fights infections and prevents cell damage, by eating a wide variety of fruits and vegetables. Eating just one orange meets most of your daily requirement. You also have the option of eating one or two servings of vitamin C rich foods, such as cantaloupe, tomatoes, sweet red pepper, broccoli, cabbage, cauliflower, white and sweet potatoes, and spinach.

Converting stored carbohydrate and other nutrients into energy is one of the many functions of vitamin B. This vitamin is involved in making red blood cells, which carry oxygen to every cell in your body. Your brain needs vitamin B for normal nerve cell communications.

The family of water-soluble vitamins includes vitamin C and B complex vitamins: thiamin, riboflavin, niacin, biotin, pantothenic acid, vitamin B6, folate, and vitamin B12. Your body needs these vitamins in small amounts to support good health. Though you may think more vitamins are better, you risk adverse health effects if you take too many vitamins and exceed the established upper levels.

Many foods contain B vitamins. Trucker-friendly foods, those that travel well, include citrus fruit, eggs, potatoes, sweet potatoes, beans, nuts, peanuts, bananas, whole grain or enriched cereals and bread, yogurt, cheese, green leafy vegetables, meat and fish.

Have you ever thought about eating foods rich in vitamin A to improve your night vision? Not only is this fat-soluble vitamin important to vision, it helps your immune system fight off infection and disease. Foods rich in vitamin A include yellow/orange fruits and vegetables (carrots, sweet potatoes, and cantaloupe), watermelon, dark green leafy vegetables, such as spinach, tomatoes, broccoli, milk and margarine. Vitamin A is packed into many delicious foods and your job is to eat them regularly.

When the sun hits the arm you are resting on the door frame, your skin is synthesizing vitamin D into usable form. Vitamin D keeps your bones and teeth strong and helps to absorb the calcium your body needs. Exposing your hands, face and arms to the sun for 10-15 minutes a few times a week will help your body process vitamin D. Check with your health care provider if you have concerns about exposing your body to sunlight.

Drinking milk is another way to get the vitamin D your body needs. Egg yolks and fatty fish are other sources of this vitamin, but go easy on the amount.

Two additional fat-soluble vitamins are vitamin E and vitamin K, which protect your body's tissues from air pollution. The sunflower seeds you enjoy so much are a good source of vitamin E, which works hand-in-hand with vitamin K to keep your body's blood clotting and ward off germs. Vitamin K is made and absorbed in your intestinal tract.

Sixty minerals – 22 of them essential – work together to keep your body functioning efficiently. Major minerals, especially sodium, chloride and potassium, keep body fluids in balance. Sodium, chloride, potassium, calcium and magnesium control your blood pressure, and direct nerve transmission and muscle contractions. Minerals play an impor-tant part in your health and you need to consume enough each day.

To get the minerals you need, choose foods from each of the five food groups. And drink plenty of water. Preventive maintenance on your truck helps you avoid costly mistakes. Eating foods rich in essential nutrients is preventive maintenance for your body.

SMART STEPS

- ✓ Eat more fruits and vegetables.
- ✓ Taste a new or different fruit or vegetable each week.

11
WATER IS
A NUTRIENT

Two thirds of the human body is water and you need to consume liquids regularly to stay hydrated. Whether it's in juice, soups, fruits, vegetables, carbonated drinks, coffee, tea, or other beverages, water impacts your health. It regulates your body temperature, helps with muscle contraction, and nerve transmission.   Water carries nutrients and energy in and out of cells, impacting diabetes, bowel regularity, risk of kidney stones, and much more. It keeps your thinking, mood and job performance at top levels.

How much water should you drink? Since your body doesn't store water, you need to drink it in one form or another to replace the water you lose when you breathe, sweat and excrete. Most people need about two quarts of water a day, or 64 ounces. The food and beverages you consume contain water, so you may not need to drink eight glasses of water a day.

There may be times – loading and unloading a truck, high altitude driving, hard exercise – when you need to drink more water. Thirst is your internal signal, a signal that tells you whether or not your body is short of water.

You may be wondering about the best water to drink. Your options include spring water, purified water, distilled water, and tap water. Spring water is water that flows naturally to the earth's surface. Mineral water contains at least 250 milligrams per liter of minerals such as magnesium and calcium. Carbon dioxide gas is added to spring water to make it sparkling water. Distillation or reverse osmosis are labeled as purified water. Sometimes distilled water is boiled and other times it is filtered.

Water is water, regardless of how it is pro-moted. Price is a factor to consider and, while tap water is free, you may not like the taste. Forty percent of the bottled water you drink started out as tap water and it is filtered through distillation, reverse osmosis, or another cleaning process. The

Environmental Pollution Administration (EPA) has standards for municipal water and tests it. In contrast, the Federal Drug Administration regulates bottled water and its standards are not as rigorous as those of the EPA. When all is said and done, you need to choose the water that you are willing to pay for and that tastes good. Evidence doesn't support the claim that bottled water is safer than tap water.

Marketers know adding vitamins, mineral and herbal supplements appeals to your sense of health. Sugars, in the forms of fructose, sucrose, fructose-glucose syrup, high fructose corn syrup, and crystalline fructose may be added to beverages to offset the taste of vitamins.

You want to quench your thirst, but may be caught off-guard by marketing claims. Nutrients and sweeteners increase the cost of beverages and throw off your plan to maintain a healthy weight.

If you're not in the habit of reading beverage labels, now is the time to start. Check the serving size first. You may think the serving size is one, when the label says it is two. Look at another beverage container where the number of servings is more than one. Assuming you will drink the entire contents, you may figure the total number of calories by multiplying the number of servings by the number of calories in one serving.

The 64-ounce supersized cola sold at fast food restaurants may lose its appeal when you realize you've consumed more than 700 calories. One pound of body weight is equal to 3,500 calories. Drinking one 64-ounce beverage a day may result in a weight gain of one pound or more per week.

Unfortunately, you may not include the calories in the beverages you drink in your daily caloric intake. If you are familiar with diabetic meal planning, you may have learned that one carb serving is 15 grams and 60 calories. A 14-ounce sugar sweetened serving of soda is approximately three servings or three carb exchanges.

Like many truckers, you may drink caffeinated beverages to stay awake. While caffeine is the desired ingredient, you may be surprised at the other cola ingredients, with sugar at the top of the list. If coffee is one of your beverage choices, keep in mind that a teaspoon of sugar is about 20 calories and a teaspoon of creamer is about the same. Depending on the creamer and sugar you add to your cup of Joe, you may be adding hundreds of calories to your daily intake.

Eating whole fruit may be more satisfying than drinking juice. If you choose juice and don't see "100% juice" on the label be wary. "Natural and artificially flavored juice" beverages contain 10 percent or less juice from concentrate. The rest of the ingredients are sugars, sweeteners, flavors, and occasionally nutri- ents. "Lite" tells you the beverage has been diluted with water. Flavored sports drinks are much the same.

Low-fat and nonfat milk and soy beverages pro- vide protein, carbohydrates, and fats, as well as vitamins and minerals: calcium, magnesium, potas- sium, zinc, iron, vitamin A, riboflavin, and folate. Drinking cow's milk, fortified soy milk, and other non-dairy drinks such as almond milk, rice milk, and grain milk should be included in moderate amounts that compliment your food plan.

Some experts prefer artificially sweetened drinks over calorically sweetened drinks because they pro- vide sweetness, but not calories. Are these sweet- eners safe? The debate continues. You may think using artificial sweeteners saves you calories, and not realize you're making up for fewer calories by eating more food.

Simple as it may seem, water is a miracle, an energy producing nutrient for your body. You can take care of your body by making water your first beverage choice.

SMART STEPS

- ✓ Bring water with you.
- ✓ Add up the dollars you save by not buying canned/bottled beverages.

12
WHAT IS
NORMAL EATING?

This case history about Larry can help you understand normal eating and choices you can make.
Larry knew he wasn't going to be able to renew his
CDL (certified drivers license) if he didn't pass the
physical. But Larry's life was complicated. Soon
after he became a commercial driver he realized his
career came with a high health cost. As his resent-
ment continued to build, his feelings of frustration
and anger increased.

Larry could feel his body changing and knew
when his blood sugar dropped. His days as an over
the road driver would be history if he couldn't figure out how to take better care of himself. He met
Kathryn during Driver Appreciation Week activities.

Sitting at a picnic table in a wide-open field, they talked about his current eating habits.

Unfortunately, he believed the stories he had heard about truckers not eating healthy. When he learned about meal planning and foods he could buy and store in his truck, he was encouraged. Making changes would help Larry to manage his hunger, weight, and diabetes. Though Larry wasn't sure he could make these positive changes, he was willing to try, and started to create a plan for positive change. Larry was desperate, and desperate times call for desperate measures.

He thought about his childhood eating. Back then, Larry ate three meals a day and snacked at regular intervals. Sitting at the family table, he was expected to eat some of all the foods that had been prepared – meat, potatoes, vegetables, fruit and dairy. He ate a wide range of foods and they satisfied his cravings for sweet, sour, bitter, tart, bland, hot, cold, creamy, crunchy and crisp. If he was still hungry after eating normal servings of each food, he ate more vegetables, had another slice of bread, or drank another glass of milk. Potato chips were a treat and soft drinks were taboo.

At the time, Larry didn't know eating three meals a day kept his blood sugar levels stable, curbed hunger pangs, and fueled his body with the right amount of energy. Despite the changes between childhood and adult life, Larry was able to see similarities between his former eating habits and the diabetes meal plan he had received.

The idea that he couldn't possibly make any changes melted away when he realized he already knew how to eat better. Learning the difference between a portion and a serving also helped Larry to maintain stable blood sugar levels and manage a stable weight. A portion is the amount of food you choose to eat. A serving is a measured amount of food based on nutrition data.

When you eat normally, you eat to satisfy hunger. You are also aware of when you start to feel full and may leave food on your plate. In other words, you learn to gauge your hunger. Before you eat, figure out where you are on the hunger scale.

Imagine a ruler in your mind and the numerals one through 10. Numeral one represents ravenous hunger and numeral 10 represents sickness. Where are you on the scale? Are you somewhere in the middle, feeling hunger pangs, or feeling satisfied, or feeling very full? Use your mental ruler to figure out how much to eat.

SMART STEPS

✓ Eat a wide range of foods each day.
✓ Determine if you are really hungry before you eat.

MEAL PLANNING
ON THE ROAD

Imagine this scene. You're parked and there is a fast food restaurant behind your truck. A shop across the street sells subway sandwiches. Three blocks way, there is a clean, well-maintained restaurant with a menu that includes heart healthy choices. A mile away, there is a grocery store with parking for big trucks.

This isn't an imaginary scene, it is often real, and means you can plan what you will eat. You can eat to live. Use your knowledge and natural skills to your advantage.

During New Driver Orientation, drivers have often said they purchased the foot-long sandwich, chips, a beverage, and a couple of cookies at a sandwich shop. Kathryn asked them to hold up their hands and list the five food groups. She asked them to compare these foods with the sandwich shop foods. How could they enhance this meal? Eating fruit, a small salad, and a carton of yogurt or drinking eight ounces of milk would create a real meal and include foods from all groups.

Instead of eating the entire sandwich, you could eat half, along with fruit, vegetables, and dairy foods, and save the other half of the sandwich for later.

Another option, Kathryn explained, is to buy Romaine lettuce, spinach, and other light-weight items at salad bars. Buying grocery store produce for less per pound – carrots, bell pepper, mushrooms, cucumbers, apples, bananas, grapes, and other items – is another option. In the bulk food aisle, you may buy nuts, sunflower seeds and other foods (in small quantities) for added variety.

Real Meals on 18 Wheels would not be complete without providing sample menus. Menu planning is simple. You may have learned it from your Mother or someone responsible for feeding you. Plan to eat every 4-6 hours to meet your body's need for energy. Eat foods from the five food groups at most meals: bread, cereal, grain, pasta group, fruit, vegetable, milk, meat and fats. Here are some breakfast ideas.

2000 Calorie Breakfast Menu

Food Group	Day 1	Day 2	Day 3	Day 4
Bread	1 c. cooked oatmeal	2 slice whole wheat toast	¾ c. shredded wheat 1 slice whole grain toast	1 English muffin
Meat	1 oz. walnuts	Vegetable omelet	1 oz. peanut butter	1 egg scrambled
Fruit	½ oz. raisins	4 oz. juice pineapple	8 oz. orange juice	1 c. fresh fruit
Milk	8 oz. low fat yogurt		8 oz. low fat milk	1 oz. low fat cheese
Fat		2 pat margarine		

More breakfast combinations:

- Two 4-inch round pancakes, 2 T. fruit spread or maple syrup, 1 tsp. butter or margarine, 1 c. 100 percent orange juice
- 1 ½ c. unsweetened flaked cereal, 1 c. low-fat or soy milk, 1 banana, 1 c. 100 percent cranberry juice
- 1 slice whole grain toast, 1 tsp. butter or margarine, 1 tsp. jelly or jam, 2 boiled eggs, ½ c. grapefruit

2000 Calorie Lunch Menu

Food Group	Day 1	Day 2	Day 3	Day 4
Bread	6" whole grain roll	2 slice grain wheat toast	2 slices whole grain bread	10 whole grain crackers
Meat	3 oz. turkey breast	3 oz. tuna	3 oz. lean ground beef	2 tbsp. peanut butter
Fruit	1 medium apple	9 large grapes	1 medium banana	1 1/2c. strawberries
Milk		8 oz. yogurt	8 oz. soy milk	8 oz. low fat milk
Vegetable	Shredded lettuce, tomato, pepper 1/2 c. beans	1 1/2 c. raw sliced vegetables: carrot celery lettuce	1 1/2 c. raw sliced vegeta-bles: tomato onion lettuce	2 c. raw vegetable salad with lettuce carrot pepper cucumber
Fat	1 tbsp. low fat mayonnaise	1 tbsp. low fat mayonnaise		2 tbsp. low fat salad dressing

More lunch combinations:

- 1 small banana, 1 cup baby carrots with low-fat dip, 1 piece of string cheese
- 1 cup chili, 5 low-fat crackers, 1 oz. low-fat cheese, salad with low-fat dressing, 4 ounces cranberry juice, 1 cup raw vegetables
- Mixed salad: greens, onion, tomato, green pepper, ½ cup garbanzo beans, 3 ounces chicken, 2 tbsp. low-fat dressing
- 6" turkey sub with vegetables, 2 cups vegetable soup, 1 fruit and cereal bar, 1 c. low-fat or soy milk

2000 Calorie Dinner Menu

Food Group	Day 1	Day 2	Day 3	Day 4
Meat	3 oz. baked fish	3 oz. top loin steak	3 oz. skinless, baked chicken	4 oz. baked salmon
Fruit			½ c. cranberry relish	
Milk	1 c. low fat milk			
Vegetable	1 c. cooked broccoli ½ c. Cole slaw 1 c. mushroom rice pilaf	½ c. green beans mixed green salad 1 c. mashed potato w/gravy	1 c. cooked carrots 1 medium baked potatoe with ¼ c. salsa	1 c. cooked spinach vegetable salad medium baked yam
Fat			2 tbsp. fat free salad dressing	

More dinner combinations:

- 1 c. pasta, 1 c. tomato sauce with ground beef, mixed green salad with low-fat dressing
- 1 ½ c. chili with lean beef, beans, tomatoes, Caesar salad (Romaine lettuce, 2 tbsp. Parmesan cheese, 1 tbsp. Caesar dressing) 1 medium apple
- Stir-fried vegetables with shrimp, 1 ½ c. cabbage, broccoli, squash cooked in olive oil, 2/3 c. brown rice, green salad with 1 tbsp. sunflower seeds and 1 tbsp. low-fat dressing
- 2 slices cheese pizza with vegetables, vegetable salad, 1 tbsp. low-fat salad dressing, 1 c. mixed fruit

Snacks

Food Group	Day 1	Day 2	Day 3	Day 4
Bread	3 rye crisp crackers		1 fruit/cereal bar	4 saltine crackers
Meat	1 oz. turkey breast slices	¼ c. almonds		1 Tbsp. peanut butter
Fruit		4 oz. cranapple juice		
Milk			1 c. low fat or soy milk	1 c. low fat or soy milk
Fat				

More snack items:

- ¾ c. dry cereal, ¼ c. sunflower seeds
- 15 reduced fat tortilla chips and ½ c. salsa
- ½ English muffin with 1 tbsp. peanut butter
- 1 medium apple with 1 c. low-fat or soy milk
- 3 c. low-fat popcorn
- 1 c. low-fat or soy milk and 1 medium fruit
- ¼ c. nuts or peanuts
- 1 low-fat or soy milk and 1 biscotti
- 1 medium fruit and 1 oz. string cheese
- 1 oz. low-fat cheese and raw vegetables: cauliflower, broccoli, carrots, pepper, mushrooms
- 4 oz. 100 percent fruit juice, ¼ c. cottage cheese, 1 medium fruit, 2 pieces rye crisp

14

TOO MUCH SALT

A doctor and a truck mechanic have two things in common. When a truck breaks down, you expect the best mechanic available to fix it. When a driver has health problems, the physician is expected to prescribe a pill or treatment plan to fix the problem. But the physician and mechanic can't prevent problems caused by neglect. A common preventable breakdown among truckers is high blood pressure, also known as hypertension.

Health experts believe one way to prevent or control hypertension is to control your salt intake and increase potassium.

In the US, one in three adults has hypertension and one in three suffer from pre-hypertension.

Higher blood pressure is called the silent killer because it has no symptoms and can go undetected for years. High blood pressure cannot be cured. Fortunately, reducing salt may be one way to lower blood pressure and lessen the risk of stroke, heart disease, heart failure, and kidney disease.

Table salt is 40 percent sodium and 60 percent chloride. Both are essential in the human body. The recommended daily intake of sodium is 1,500 to 2,300 milligrams a day, or about one teaspoon. One teaspoon isn't very much and most Americans are eating two-to-three times more salt than they need. This salt comes from canned foods, processed foods (like deli meats), and restaurant food, especially fast food restaurants.

Sodium makes food taste better and acts as a preservative. It is often a hidden ingredient in broth, soup, cocktail sauce, salsa, ketchup, dips, beef jerky, chips, cured meats, and Asian food. Depending on your health, it may be wise to steer clear of these foods.

Excess sodium in the diet may not be the only culprit in high blood pressure. Insufficient potassium and calcium may contribute to high blood pressure. Potassium works with sodium to regulate the body's water balance. The recommended intake of potassium for adults is 4,700 milligrams per day. The more potassium and less sodium you have each day, the greater the likelihood of lowering blood pressure. But this doesn't mean a person with high blood pressure should take potassium supplements.

The following chart gives you an idea of the sodium and potassium content of foods.

Sodium and Potassium Content of Foods

Food	Amount *	Potassium Mg **	Sodium Mg ***
Bacon	3 slices	100	300–500
Bologna	2 oz.	75–125	600–800
Cheese, natural	1–1 ½ oz.	30–60	110–450
Cheese, processed	1 oz.	45–60	400
Chips,	1 oz.	35–60	100–200
Dressing, Salad	1 T	trace	75–220
Fruit, fresh, frozen, canned	**½ c.**	**160–450**	**Trace**
Ketchup, mustard, steak sauce	1 T	Trace	130–230
Meat, poultry, fish, Fresh	3 oz.	200–350	< 90
Milk, low fat	8 oz.	350–500	120
Peanuts, roasted, salted	1 oz.	200	120
Potato, baked, boiled unsalted	1 med	>500	Trace
Pretzels, salted	1 oz.	40–80	130–880
Tomato, raw	1 med	300	Trace
Tomato juice canned	¾ c.	350-500	660
Vegetables, fresh, cooked frozen, unsalted	**½ c.**	**160**	**< 70**
Vegetables, fresh, canned, frozen with sauce	½ c.	200–350	140–460
Yogurt	8 oz.	350–500	160

* c=cup oz.=ounce tsp.=teaspoon T=tablespoon

>= more than *<=less than

Substituting fruits and vegetables for sodium is a simple way to combat hypertension. Remember, fruits and vegetables are naturally low in sodium and high in potassium. Your mother's order to "eat your vegetables" is still good advice. You can improve this advice by not adding salt to food and, if you cook on the road, substituting herbs and spices for salt. Without salt, you are able to taste the true flavors of nature's bounty.

SMART STEPS

- ✓ Push the salt shaker away and cut back on high salt condiments.
- ✓ Ask the cook to hold the salt.

YOUR NUTRITION NUMBERS

You'll be surprised at how fast you gain insight into your eating habits by using these resources. You may record what you eat and compare your notes with the recommendations in this book. Or you may compare what you eat or drink for part of your day, a single meal, or snacks with your estimated needs.

Make changes gradually. Cut back on some foods and eliminate others. Enjoy the taste of each food you eat and find pleasure in trying new ones. If you have a prescribed meal plan and find it challenging, now may be the time to ask for help. Consult a pharmacist if you are unsure of how prescribed medications interact with foods. Here is a step-by-step guide to healthy eating on the highway.

1. Calculate your estimated calorie needs.

Your **current** weight: _____ + 0 = _____ calories.

Your **desired** weight: _____ + 0 = _____ calories.

Divide your estimated calorie needs by 3 for an estimate of calories to consume every 4-6 hours. Example: 200 + 0 = 2,000 calories divided by 3 = 666 calories.

As you begin, use your current body weight as a comparison point. Once you know your current habits, compare them with your recommendations. Identify the changes you can make.

2. Calculate your estimated daily needs for carbohydrate, protein and fat.

Write your estimated calorie needs here. _____

Our calculations are based on a 2,000 calorie need with 50 percent from carbohydrate, 20 percent from protein, and less than 30 percent from fat. To bypass the calculations, proceed to the Quick Reference below.

3. Calculate your carbohydrate needs based on 50 percent of total daily calories.

Your estimated total daily calorie needs: _____

x .50 = _____ calories from carbohydrate.

Your estimated calories from carbohydrate: _____ divided by 4 = _____ grams.

Divide your total daily calories from carbohydrate by 3 to estimate carbohydrate needs every 4–6 hours. Example:

Total calories: 2,000 x .50 = 1,000 calories from carbohydrate.

Divide by 4 (4 calories per gram) = 250 grams.

Divide 1,000 by 3 = 333 calories and 250 by 3 = 83 grams every 4–6 hours.

Note: This is the information used to calculate calories in diabetic meal plans. In diabetes carbo-hydrate counting 1 carb exchange = 60 calories/15 grams. In a 2,000 calorie diabetic meal, this plan translates into 5.6 carbs every 4-6 hours. You may want to ask your diabetes educator to review your meal plan with you.

4. Calculate your protein needs based on 20 percent of total daily calories.

Your daily calorie needs are _____ x .20 = _____ calories from protein.

Your estimated calories from protein are _____ divided by 4 (4 calories per gram) = _____ grams.

Divide your daily calories from protein by 3 to estimate protein needs every 4–6 hours. Example:

Total calories: 2,000 x .20 = 400 calories from protein.

Divide by 4 (4 calories per gram) = 100 grams.

Divide 400 by 3 = 133 calories and 133 by 3 = 33 grams every 4–6 hours.

5. Calculate your fat needs based on less than 30 percent of total daily calories.

Your estimated daily calorie needs are _____ x .30 = _____ calories from protein.

Your estimated calories from fat are _____ divided by 9 (9 calories per gram) = _____ grams.

Divide your daily calories from fat by 3 to estimate fat needs every 4–6 hours. Example:

Total calories: 2,000 x .30 = 600 calories from fat.

Divide by 9 (9 calories per gram) = 67 grams.

Divide by 3 for intake every 4–6 hours = 200 calories, 22 grams of fat.

The Quick Reference on the next page tells you more about your energy needs for protein, carbohydrate and fat.

Quick Reference

In recommended ranges of
Protein 10-35%; Carbohydrate 45-65%; and Fat at less than 30%

	1500	1800	2100	2400	2700
If your calorie needs are:					
Then a desirable daily protein intake range in calories is:	150–350	180–630	210–735	240–840	270–945
And in gram is:	38–88	45–157	68–184	60–210	68–236
Then a desirable daily carbohydrate intake range in calories is:	675–975	810–1170	945–1365	1080–1560	1215–1755
And in grams is:	168–243	202–292	236–341	270–390	303–439
A desirable daily fat intake in calories is less than:	450	540	630	720	810
And in grams is less than:	50	60	70	80	90

Sources of Carbohydrate, Protein and Fat in Food by Food Groups			
Food Group	**Carbohydrate**	**Protein**	**Fat**
Grain	***	*	-
Vegetables	***	-	*
Fruit	***	-	-
Milk	***	***	varies
Meat & Beans	varies	varies	varies
Oils			***

Key: *** denotes major source,* some but not major source, - none, varies amounts vary.

Resource: http://www.nal.usda.gov/fnic/foodcomp/ Data/HG72/hg72.html

TO YOUR HEALTH!

There's a lot of information in this guide, but it won't improve your health unless you use it. When all is said and done, you are in charge of you. You are the only one who can change your life. Though your health hinges partly on genetics and lifestyle, you can take steps to improve it.

Healthy living on the road can improve your driving and prolong your life. As one trucker said, "I'm eating healthy for my grandchildren."

Change is a series of baby steps. Each step, small as it may be, keeps you on the path to better health. When changes are new, you have to keep reminding yourself about them. But as time passes these changes will become automatic. In fact, the changes you make may become life affirmations.

You cut back on portion sizes. You choose to eat healthy foods regularly. You stop going back for second and thirds. You push the salt shaker away. You drink less caffeine. You consume less sugar. You read food labels. You build physical activity into your days.

Though we can't be in the cab with you, we are with you in spirit and cheering for you. We want you to succeed, so here are our best tips for healthy living on the highway.

1   Remember why healthy eating is important.
2   Plan menus, make a list, and purchase food to eat in your truck.
3   Eat when you are hungry. Stop when you are satisfied. It's okay to leave food on your plate and ask for a "to go" box.
4   Get enough sleep.
5   Put physical activity on your schedule.
6   Order baked, grilled or steamed food.
7   Eat fruits and vegetables every day.
8   Use information on food labels to make food and beverage choices.
9   Make water your first beverage choice.
10 Enjoy treats in moderation.

We are eager to receive your feedback. Post your comments – especially your success stories – on www.realmealson18wheels.com. Your comments could help other commercial drivers. Here's to your health and longevity!

APPENDIX A: WORKSHEET

Worksheet

Your Daily Calorie Needs _____

Protein - 20% _____ **4 calories = 1 gram**

Carbohydrate -50% _____ **4 calories = 1 gram**

Fat less than -30% _____ **9 calories = 1 gram**

Food Group	Food – Beverage Item	Portion	Total Calories	Protein Calories or Grams	Carbohydrate Calories or Grams	Fat Calories or Grams
Meat-Beans						
Vegetable						
Fruit						
Grain						
Milk						
Totals						
Meat-Beans						
Vegetable						
Fruit						
Grain						
Milk						
Totals						
Meat-Bean						
Vegetable						
Fruit						
Grain						
Milk						
Snack						
Total						
Daily Total						

APPENDIX B: NUTRITIVE VALUE OF FOODS

Volume and Weight Equivalents

Volumes

Level Measure	Equivalent	Metric
1 gallon (gal)	4 quarts	3.786 liter/3786 millileter
1 quart (qt.)	4 cups	.946 liter/946 millileter
1 cup (c.)	8 fluid ounces ½ pint (pt.) 16 tablespoons	237 millileter
1 tablespoons (tbsp.)	1 fluid ounce	30 millileter

Weights

Level Measure	Equivalent	Metric
1 pound (lb.)	16 ounces (oz.)	453.6 grams (gm)
1 ounce 9 (oz)		28.36 grams
3 ½ ounces		100 grams

Use Nutritive Values of Food as a guide to understanding where the calories and nutrients are provided in food. Understanding where the protein, carbohydrates and fats are provided will give you meal planning insight. How much should you eat? That depends on how many calories you need. Age, sex, size, and how active you are determine your needs. Recalling the recommendation to eat a fist-size portion from each food group may help you to eat normally and not over eat. As you plan your food for the day, you may find the following recommendations helpful.

Grains: 6–11 servings

Vegetables: 3–5 servings

Fruit: 2–5 servings

Milk: 2–3 servings

Meats/Beans: 2–3 servings

Fats: 2–3 servings

Sweets: 5 per week

A complete list of the Nutritive Values of Foods may be found at the US Dept. of Agriculture, Agricultural Research Service, 2010. USDA National Nutrient Database for Standard Reference, Release 23. Nutrient Data Laboratory Home Page, http://www.ars.usda.gov/ba/bhnrc/ndl.

When you search for nutritive values of food on the Internet, use the words "nutritional value." For example, milk, nutritional value. Here are some examples of the Nutritive Value of Foods in each of the food groups.

Grains:

Plan to eat 6–11 servings per day. What is a serving? The following chart gives you some examples. Most of your choices should be low-fat and low-sugar, things like bread, English muffins, rice and pasta. Go easy on spreads, seasonings and toppings. One serving of grains can be a slice of bread, half cup of rice, cooked cereal, or pasta, one cup of ready-to-eat cereal, or one flat tortilla.

Nutritive Values of Grains

Food Item	Serving	Energy in calories	Protein in grams	Carbohydrate in grams	Fat in grams
Bagel	3-inch round	165	6	28	2
Bread, white	1 oz. slice	70	2	13	1
Bread, wheat	1 oz. slice	65	3	14	1
Oatmeal, cooked	1 c.	130	5	23	2
Ready to eat cereal Shredded wheat	½ c.	90	2	20	1
Crackers, saltine	4 crackers	55	1	10	1
Cookie, Chocolate chip	4–2 ¼"	200	2	29	9
Donut, glazed	3 ¾" x 1 ¼"	200	3	22	11
Muffin, bran	1 oz. 2 3/8" x 1 ½"	105	3	17	4
Noodles, cooked	1 c.	200	7	37	2
Pizza, cheese	4 ¾" of 12" diameter	145	6	22	4
Spaghetti, cooked	1 c.	190	7	39	1
Pancakes, plain	4"diameter	55	2	6	2

Fruits:

Plan 2–5 servings of fruit each day from the rainbow of colors nature has provided: orange, purple, yellow, red, white and green. Fruit may satisfy your sweet tooth and is naturally low in fat, sodium, and calories. One serving of fruit can be a medium apple, one orange, one banana, a half cup of fresh, frozen, cooked or canned fruit, a half cup of fruit juice, or a quarter cup of dried fruit. See the chart on the next page for more information about fruit servings and their nutritional values.

Nutritive Values of Fruit

Food Item	Serving	Energy In calories	Protein In grams	Carbohydrate In grams	Fat In grams
Apple, raw	1 – 2 ¾"	80	-	20	-
Apple juice, bottled or canned	½ c.	60	-	15	-
Banana, peeled	½ c.	50	-	13	-
Cantaloupe	½ of 5" melon	80	2	20	-
Grape Thompson, seedless	10 grapes	35	-	9	-
Orange, whole	1-2 5/8'	65	1	16	-
Orange juice, raw	½ c.	55	1	13	-
Pineapple, raw, diced	1 c.	80	1	21	-
Pineapple, juice, unsweetened	½ c.	70	-	17	-
Raisins, seedless	½ oz. packet	40	-	11	-
Strawberries, raw	1 c.	55	1	13	-
Watermelon, raw	4" x 8 " wedge	110	2	27	-

Vegetables:

Plan 3–5 servings of vegetables from a range of colors and textures each day, dark green, orange, crunchy and smooth. A variety of textures, colors and flavors enhances your feeling of being satisfied. Most vegetables are very low in calories and rich in essential nutrients.

One serving of vegetables is one cup of raw, leafy vegetables, ½ cup raw or cooked vegetables, ¾ cup vegetable juice, one small potato or sweet potato. See the chart on the next page for more information about the nutritive values of vegetables.

Nutritive Values of Vegetables

Food Item	Serving	Energy In calories	Protein In grams	Carbohydrate In grams	Fat In grams
Beans, green, raw Frozen, canned	1 c.	30	2	7	-
Broccoli, cooked	1 c.	40	5	7	-
Cabbage, shredded	1 c.	15	1	4	-
Carrots, raw	1 – 7 ½ "	30	1	7	-
Carrots, cooked	1 c.	50	1	11	1
Cauliflower, raw or cooked	1 c.	30	3	6	-
Corn, sweet, kernels	½ c.	65	2	15	1
Cucumber, slices	6-8 slices	5	-	-	-
Lettuce, raw	1 c.	10	-	2	-
Potatoes, mashed	½ c	80	3	15	-
Potatoes, baked	3 oz.– ¼ large	80	3	15	-
Potatoes, French fries	10- 2-3 ½"	135	2	18	7
Squash, Winter, cooked	1 c.	80	3	15	-
Tomato, raw or canned	1 raw ½ c.	25	1	6	-
Yam, baked	½ c.	80	1	15	-

Meat and Beans:

Plan to eat 4–7 ounces of meat, poultry or fish a day. You may substitute dried beans for protein. Your choices should be lean or low-fat. One serving is an ounce of meat, poultry or fish, one egg, one tablespoon of peanut butter, half an ounce of nuts or seeds, or half a cup of dried beans. See the chart on the next age for more information about the nutritive value of meat and beans.

Nutritive Values of Meat and Beans

Food Item	Serving	Energy In calories	Protein In grams	Carbohydrate In grams	Fat In grams
Beef, ground 80% lean	3 oz.	235	20	-	17
Beef, cooked, pot roast	3 oz.	245	23	-	16
Beef, sirloin, broiled	3 oz.	330	20		27
Beef, vegetable stew	1 cup	220	16	15	11
Chili with beans	1 cup	340	19	31	16
Pork, Ham, cured, cooked	3 oz.	245	18	-	19
Pork, luncheon meat, Boiled ham	1 oz.	65	5	-	5
Pork, chop, loin lean & fat	3 oz.	310	21	-	24
Pork, sausage	1 oz.	140	6	-	6
Egg, large, raw	1	80	6	1	6
Egg, scrambled, milk added Also omelet	1	95	6	1	7
Chicken, breast, meat only	3 oz.	140	26	-	3
Chicken, Meat, & skin, Fried with batter	3 oz.	221	21	8	11
Chicken and noodles	1 cup	365	22	26	17
Fish, Haddock, fried	3 oz.	140	17	-	5
Tuna, canned in oil drained solids	3 oz.	170	24	-	7
Salmon	3 oz.	120	17	-	5
Beans, Cooked, Great northern, navy, red kidney	1 cup	230	15	40	1
Nuts, almond 20-24 pieces	1 oz.	160	6	6	14
Nuts, cashew 16-18 pieces	1 oz.	160	4	10	13
Nuts, walnuts 14 halves	1 oz.	190	4	5	18
Seeds, Sunflower	¼ cup	200	9	7	17
Peanut, butter	1 Tbsp.	95	4	3	8
Tofu, raw firm,	4 oz. ½ cup	94	10	-	5
Hummus	¼ cup	102	5	8	6

Milk, Dairy and Milk Substitutes:

Plan 2–3 servings a day. Fluid milk products and many foods made from milk are included in this group. Your choices should be fat-free or low-fat. Calcium is retained in the processing of fluid milk, but much is lost in processed foods including cottage cheese, yogurt and cheese. One serving from the dairy group can be a half cup of milk or yogurt, one and half ounces of natural cheese, or two ounces of processed cheese. See the chart on the next page for more information about the nutritive values of milk and milk substitutes.

Nutritive Values of Milk and Milk Substitutes

Food Item	Serving	Energy In calories	Protein In grams	Carbohydrate In grams	Fat In grams
Butter, Regular,	1 tbsp.	100	-	-	12
Butter, 1"square x 1/3"	1 pat	35	-	-	4
Cheese, Cheddar	1 oz.	122	8	-	10
Cheese, Mozzarella, whole milk	1 oz.	90	6	-	7
Cheese, Mozzarella, Part skim milk	1 oz.	80	8		5
Cheese, fat free, White or yellow	1 oz.	30	5	2	-
Pasteurized process cheese; American	1 oz.	105	6	-	9
Pasteurized process cheese; Swiss	1 oz.	95	7	1	7
Cheese, cottage 4%	1 c.	235	28	6	10
Cheese, cottage 1%	1 c.	165	28	6	2
Cream, Ice cream Regular 16% fat	1 c.	350	4	32	24
Ice Milk, 4.3% fat	1 c.	185	5	29	6
Cream, sour	1tbsp.	30	-	1	3
Milk, substitute with Hydr. Vegetable Oils	1 c.	150	4	15	8
Milk, whole 3.3%	1 c.	150	8	11	8
Milk, Reduced fat 2%	1 c.	121	8	12	5
Milk, Low fat 1%	1 c.	102	8	12	3
Milk, fat-free –skim	1 c.	86	8	12	0
Milk, chocolate 2%	1 c.	179	8	26	5
Yogurt, plain, whole milk	1 c.	139	8	11	7
Yogurt, plain, fat-free	1 c.	120	13	17	0
Yogurt, frozen	½ c.	160	3	27	6

Oils:

Because oils such as those found in fish, nuts and vegetables containing fatty acids for essential health, there is an allowance in our meal plan. Check food labels to guide your choices. Vegetable oils include canola, corn, cottonseed, olive, peanut, safflower, soybean, and sunflower. The amounts: 1 tablespoon, 3 teaspoons, or 14 grams. The approximate calories from fat: 120. The following US Government Food Pyramid chart has more information about the nutritive value of oils.

Nutritive Values of Oils

Food Item	Serving (Tablespoon)	Energy in calories	Protein in grams	Carbohydrate in grams	Fat In grams
Oil, Canola, corn, olive, pea-nut, safflower, sunflower, soybean, or cottonseed	1 Tbsp.	120	-	-	14
Bacon, cooked	1 slice	85	4	-	8
Butter, Peanut*	2 Tbsp.	190	8	7	16
Peanuts, dry roasted*	1 oz.	175	7	7	15
Almonds, dry roasted*	1 oz.	175	7	7	15
Seeds, sunflower*	1 oz.	175	7	7	15
Mayonnaise	1 Tbsp.	100	-	-	11
Dressing, Regular Thousand Island	1 Tbsp.	80	-	2	8
Dressing, low fat Thousand Island	1 Tbsp.	25	-	2	2
Dressing, Regular French,	1 Tbsp.	65		3	6
Dressing, low fat French	1 Tbsp.	15	-	2	1
Butter	1 Tbsp.	100	-	-	12
Butter, pat	1¼"x 1/3"	35	-	1	4

*nuts, seeds and peanuts are part of the protein food group

Sweets:

Sugar may be added to foods and beverages in processing or preparation, adding calories and limited nutrients. However, sugar found naturally in fruits and milk, in limited amounts, may not be a problem. Most of the added sugar in your diet comes from:

- Carbonated drinks
- Candy
- Cakes
- Pies
- Fruit punch, lemonade
- Ice cream
- Pudding
- Sweetened yogurt
- Sweetened milk
- Sweet rolls and cinnamon toast

The names for added sugars on food labels include brown sugar, corn sweetener, corn syrup, dextrose, fructose, fruit juice concentrates, glucose, high-fructose corn syrup, honey, invert sugar, lactose, maltose, malt syrup, molasses, raw sugar, sucrose, sugar, and syrup.

Sources:

http://www.choosemyplate.gov/foodgroupsemptycalories_
sugars.html
US Dept. of Agriculture, Agricultural Research Service,
2005. USDA National Nutrient Database for Standard
Reverence, Release 18. Nutrient Data Laboratory Home
Page, http://www.ars.usda.gov/ba/bhnrc/ndl

ABOUT THE AUTHORS

Kathryn Clements has been a registered dietitian for 20 years. Throughout her career, she stayed focused on the importance of nutrition to promote health. She facilitated one of the first worksite health promotion programs, piloted a program at Malt-O-Meal and, ultimately, within the trucking industry.

She has presented nutrition information at driver orientation sessions, safety meetings, and Diver Appreciation Week. Her nutrition articles have appeared in national, state, and local trucking publications. Clements lives in Cannon Falls, Minnesota and is the owner and CEO of Clements Health Consulting, LLC. Visit www.realmealson18wheels.com for more information or to post your comments.

ℬ

Harriet Hodgson has been an independent journalist for more than 30 years. She is a member of the American Society of Journalists and Authors, Association of Health Care Journalists, and Association for Death Education and Counseling.

A popular speaker, Hodgson has given presentations at Alzheimer's, hospice, and health conferences. She has appeared on more than 160 radio talk shows, including CBS, and dozens of television stations, including CNN.

Her work is cited in the **World Who's Who of Women**, **Who's Who of American Women**, **Who's Who in America**, **Contemporary Authors**, and other directories. Hodgson is a GRG – grandparent raising grandchildren – and lives in Rochester, Minnesota with her husband John and her twin grandchildren. Please visit www.harriethodgson.com for more information about this busy author and grandmother.

CPSIA information can be obtained at www.ICGtesting.com
Printed in the USA
LVOW130739050812

292955LV00007B/31/P